SOMETIMES
Bad Things
HAPPEN

Ellen Jackson
Photographs by Shelley Rotner

THE MILLBROOK PRESS
BROOKFIELD, CONNECTICUT

Sometimes
bad things
happen. You
may feel sad,
scared, hurt,
or angry.

Your game is
canceled
because of rain.

Your brother tells
you that a
bully pushed him.

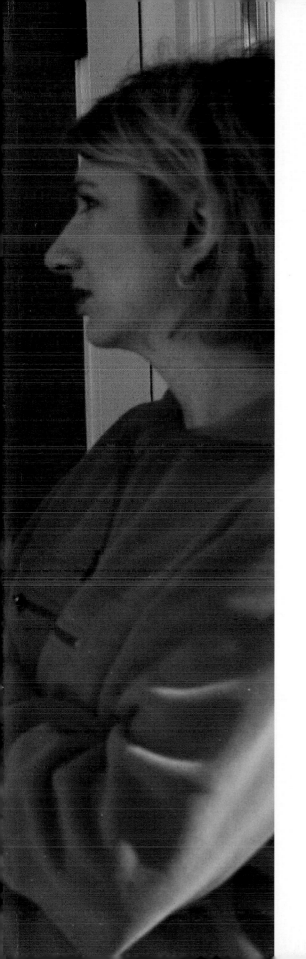

Grown-ups fight.

You see scary
news stories on
television.

A few people do
bad things.

But most people
want to make
the world a
better place for
everyone.

These people
build homes for
the homeless.

They rescue
people who
have been hurt.

They care for
animals.

Or help children
feel safe.

Kick a ball.

Look up at the sky.

Sing a brave song.

Help someone.

It's okay to cry.
And very soon . . .

When you are
sad, scared, hurt,
or angry, think
about the good
people you know.

When bad things
happen . . .

Hug a friend.

Plant a flower.

Listen to a poem.